ANGRY BIRDS STAR WARS™

LARD VADER'S VILLAINS

Written by Ruth Amos

LONDON, NEW YORK, MUNICH,
MELBOURNE and DELHI

Editorial Assistant Ruth Amos
Senior Editor Elizabeth Dowsett
Senior Designer Lynne Moulding
Jacket Designer Lynne Moulding
Pre-production Producer Marc Staples
Producer Charlotte Oliver
Managing Editor Laura Gilbert
Design Manager Maxine Pedliham
Art Director Ron Stobbart
Publishing Director Simon Beecroft

Reading Consultant Maureen Fernandes

Lucasfilm
Executive Editor J. W. Rinzler
Art Director Troy Alders
Keeper of the Holocron Leland Chee
Director of Publishing Carol Roeder

Rovio
Approvals Editor Nita Ukkonen
Senior Graphic Designer Jan Schulte-Tigges
Content Manager Laura Nevanlinna
Vice President of Book Publishing Sanna
Lukander

First published in Great Britain in 2013 by
Dorling Kindersley Limited
80 Strand, London WC2R 0RL

10 9 8 7 6 5 4 3
007–193695–Mar/2013

Page design copyright © 2013 Dorling Kindersley Limited

Angry Birds™ © 2009–2013 Rovio Entertainment Ltd.
All rights reserved.
© 2013 Lucasfilm Ltd. LLC & ® or TM where indicated.
All rights reserved. Used under authorisation.

A CIP catalogue record for this book
is available from the British Library.

ISBN: 978-1-40933-309-8

Colour reproduction by Altaimage, UK
Printed and bound in China by L.Rex

Discover more at
www.dk.com
www.starwars.com

Contents

STAR WARS

LARD VADER'S VILLAINS

Written by Ruth Amos

The Pork Side

This is a very wicked
gang of pigs!
The pigs belong to the
Pig Empire and they
love to guzzle junk food.

Emperor
Piglatine

Lard Vader

The pigs are trying to find the legendary Egg, which holds the power to rule the galaxy. First they must defeat the Bird Rebels, who are defending the Bird Republic. The birds want to be left in peace, but the pigs want power!

Boba Fatt

Pigtrooper

Guard

Lard Vader

Lard Vader is one of the
Pig Empire's chiefs.
His greatest ambition is to
find the mysterious Egg.

A long time ago he was a
Jedi, but then he joined the pigs.
The Jedi are warriors who serve
and protect the Bird Republic.

Lard Vader wants to be the most important pig, so he likes to stand on his Pigtrooper soldiers to seem taller. Unfortunately, he often falls off!

Pigtrooper

Another Pigtrooper!

Emperor Piglatine

Emperor Piglatine is the leader of the Pig Empire.

He rules over all the other pigs in the galaxy.

Hidden weapon

The Emperor has banned all delicious junk food and sweets in the galaxy, so that he can gobble it all down by himself.

Emperor Piglatine is not a very pretty pig – he has droopy green skin and a slimy snout. Luckily, the rest of his face is covered by a hood!

Lightsabers
The Emperor and his pigs fight with red lightsaber weapons. Bird Rebel warriors use blue ones.

The Emperor's guards

These guards are Emperor Piglatine's personal piggy protection. They are supposed to follow behind the Emperor at all times to protect him.

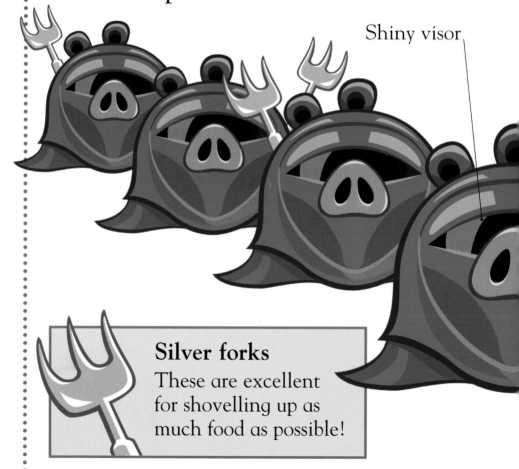

Shiny visor

Silver forks
These are excellent for shovelling up as much food as possible!

Unfortunately, they are too busy tripping over each other's long robes to protect him!

The guards carry forks to help them deliver junk food and sweets to their greedy leader.

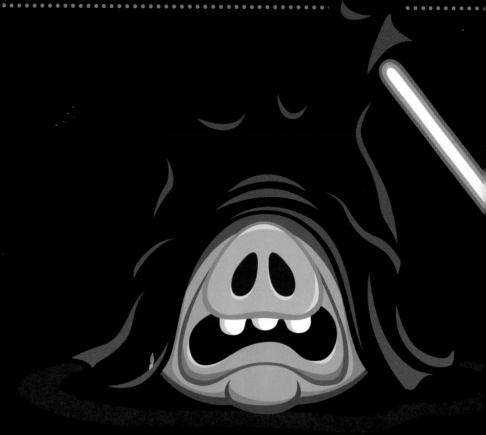

Duel for piggy power

Emperor Piglatine has no idea that Lard Vader wants to be the leader of the pigs. Porky Piglatine is too busy eating as much food as possible to notice.

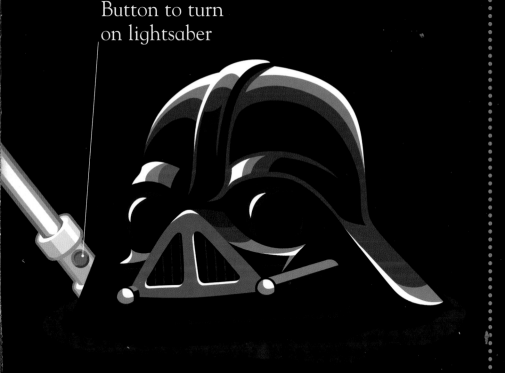

Button to turn
on lightsaber

Lard Vader often tries
to sneak up on the Emperor
with his lightsaber.
The Emperor thinks it is a
silly joke and just laughs at him!
Vader still hopes to be top pig.

Pigtroopers

Attention! This squadron
of Pigtroopers are Emperor
Piglatine's soldiers.
The Pigtroopers must search
the galaxy for junk food and
bring it back to the Emperor.

Triangle-shaped snout

Unfortunately, these soldier swine are utterly useless at their job – they often get lost. They hate asking for directions and they are not very good at using their snouts to sniff out clues.

Hard helmet

The Bird Rebels

Squawk! Look who it is!
This fantastic flock is called
the Bird Rebels.
These heroic adventurers must
fight to save the galaxy from the
wicked pigs.

Chuck
"Ham"
Solo

Terebacca

Red
Skywalker

Lard Vader and his villainous
friends keep trying to defeat the
birds, but they are too brave
and clever!

C-3PYOLK

R2-EGG2

Obi-Wan
Kaboomi

Princess
Stella
Organa

Yoda
Bird

17

The Pig Star

Behold, the Pig Star!
The Pig Empire has built
an incredible new super
weapon, which has the
power to blow up the
entire universe!
The Pig Star has big ears
and a round snout, just
like the pigs.

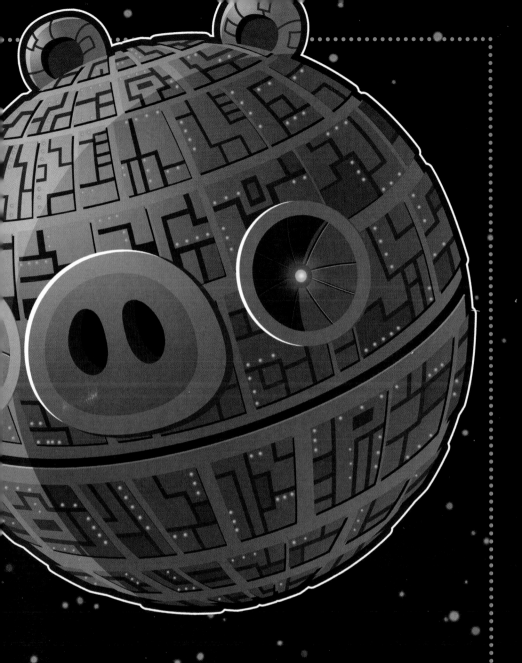

The Bird Rebels are terrified
by the Pig Star's scary face –
even Princess Stella.

Jabba and bounty hunters

Monstrous Jabba the Hog
is a wicked crime lord who
secretly sells junk food.
He often buys sweets from the
food smuggler and Bird Rebel,
Ham Solo.

Jabba the
Hog

Slug-like
tail

Jabba likes to work with other sneaky crooks. He pays bounty hunter pigs to track down birds who have escaped, in exchange for a big sack of treats. This bounty hunter has bulging eyes for spotting runaway birds!

Bounty hunter

Boba Fatt

Boba Fatt is another
bounty hunter.
Lard Vader pays Boba to zoom
around the galaxy on his jet pack
and find the
Mighty Falcon.

Antenna
for receiving
messages

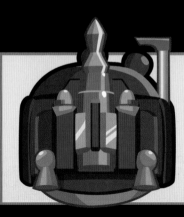

Jet pack
Boba's bright blue and
orange jet pack propels
him through space on
his missions.

The *Falcon* is Ham Solo's
fantastic starship.
Ham gives the Bird Rebels a ride
in it when they go on quests.
Boba tries to stop the *Falcon*.
He wants to take the birds back
to Lard Vader, who will give
him lots of sweets to slurp!

Imperial army

Lard Vader has different kinds of pigs to fight for the Empire. The pigs in white helmets are called Snowtroopers, and they wear special masks to shield their snouts from the cold.

Pig Pilot

Pig Empire
symbol

The Pig Pilots who wear black
armour are in charge of zooming
around the galaxy in aircraft.
The Pig Commanders in white
have red Pig Empire symbols on
their helmets, and they give out
silly orders to the Pigtroopers.

The Egg

This is The Egg that Lard Vader
and his villains want!

The Egg contains the Force –
a form of energy that has the
power to rule the universe.

Yoda Bird disguised The Egg as
the bird droid, R2-EGG2,
to keep it safe.

Yoda Bird, Red Skywalker and
Obi-Wan Kaboomi are Jedi
warriors, who study the Force
to defend the Bird Republic.
Red and Obi-Wan use the Force
to try to find The Egg.
Unfortunately, old Yoda Bird
keeps forgetting to tell the
other Jedi where he hid it!

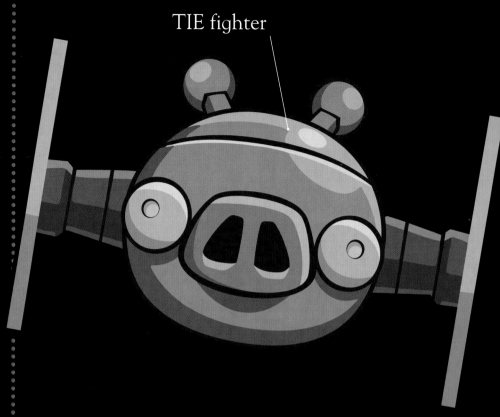

TIE fighter

Villainous vehicles

The wicked Pig Pilots have plenty of vehicles they use to carry out their pig patrols. The pigs fly TIE fighter aircraft with bulging eyes and big grins.

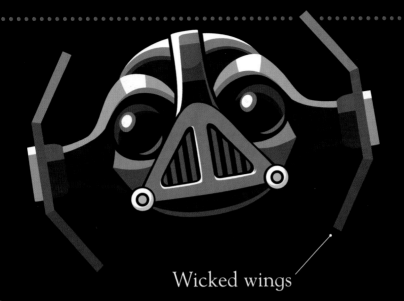

Wicked wings

Lard Vader has his own
fast, personalised TIE fighter
with glowing red eyes.
He expects all the other
TIE fighters to move out
of the way for him!

Breathing tubes
The Pig Pilots' masks
have special breathing
equipment to help
them breathe in space.

Big battle

On the frozen planet of Hoth, Lard Vader's villains ambush these cross birds!

The Pig Commanders ride huge AT-AT walkers across the snow. Luckily, the Bird Rebels defend themselves fiercely.

Red strikes with his lightsaber
and Ham Solo fires his blaster.

Victory to the Bird Rebels!
Lard Vader and the Pig Empire
must try again
another day...

AT-AT
walker

Quiz

1. Who is the leader of the Pig Empire?

2. What is the name of this vehicle?

3. Whose side is Red Skywalker on?

4. What is this super weapon called?

5. Where is The Egg hidden?

Index